The Giving Sack

Jeanne Hill
2019.

Piece of Cake
PUBLISHING

A CHRISTMAS TRADITION

The Giving Sack

Written & Illustrated by Leanne E. Hill

FOR MORE JOY SPREADING TIPS, PLEASE VISIT WWW.THEGIVINGSACK.COM

In memory of my dad & for my children

"i carry your heart with me
(i carry it in my heart)"
— *e.e. cummings*

Hello there.

If I could shake your hand I would—so please consider this an "air shake." Thank you so much for bringing my book and tradition into your home. I hope it becomes a small and joyful part of your holiday season.

Please know that in simply purchasing this book, you are already giving back! *The Giving Sack - Give Back* donates 3% of our annual sales directly back to the UMFS Scholarship Fund, which has provided hundreds of children in foster care financial aid toward continuing their education after high school. Please visit our website to learn more about this beautiful resource.

I wrote this book to give life to a delightful tradition. The act of giving toys is nothing new, but delivering the message in the form of a refreshing visual story is. I have three hopes for this little book. The first is this book will gently encourage the hearts of little people to be excited about giving and helping those in need. Secondly, I imagine this book being used as a beginner's tool in discussing economic diversity with children in a way easily comprehended by young minds. In doing so, it gives those children a responsibility and an understanding that they have the power to positively make a difference in the lives of another through simple acts of generosity and servitude. My final hope is that this story becomes a fun and magical tradition to share with your family for years to come. I hope it renews the true meaning of Christmas within your home. I wish that you receive as much joy and warmth in this tradition as my own family does. And, hey… let's be real, if it can help parents clean out their children's rooms before the holiday season, then that is just an extra bonus.

Inserted in this book you will find simple instructions on how to execute this tradition. The directions are vague on purpose. I want this to be an easy tradition—do whatever makes this fun, easy and effective for your family. Visit our website to find tips and other ways to spread the joy of giving with *The Giving Sack*.

From my family to yours, Merry Christmas.

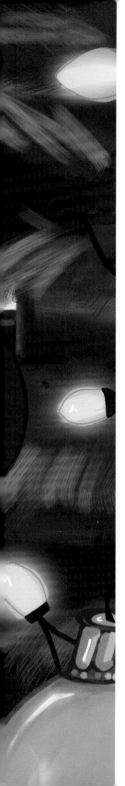

Greetings to you little one
The time is coming near,

Christmas will be arriving soon

with all its gifts and cheer.

You see, around the world

Both far and near

There are children who do not receive

Like you, during this time of year.

There are children whose dinner plates
Are not always full of delicious food to eat,
Children whose homes aren't as warm
And children with holes in the shoes
on their feet.

Me and the elves we do our best

To give kids all they need

But, we need your help and are asking you

For a kind and generous deed.

I've given you a magic sack
Made of thread from my
Christmas coat.

I've sprinkled it with magic dust

A mixture of love and hope.

Please fill it with your once loved toys

That no longer have a place.

Broken wheels, missing pieces

Or simply no longer fit your taste.

Place the sack
on your front step
And be sure to
bundle it tight

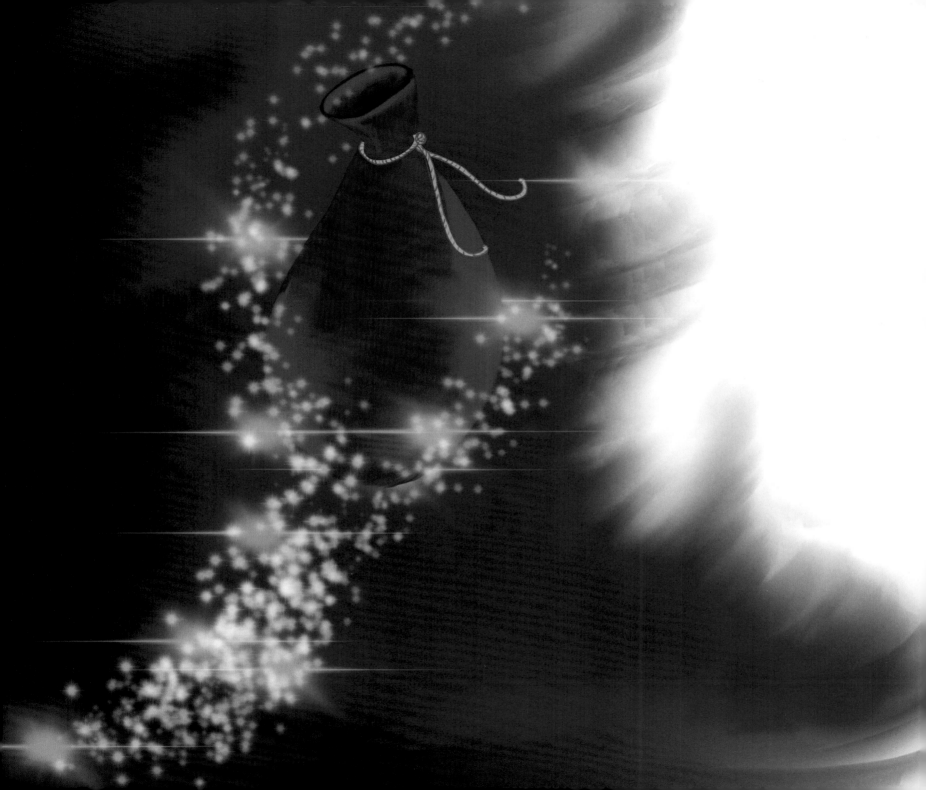

For, from the magic dust...

Your sack takes flight at night!

The sacks travel from all around the world

High up in the clouds

Until they reach the North Pole
Where they will gently touch the ground.

I'll fix your toys
and mend them,
Making them
all brand new.
I will then
deliver them
to good little children
less fortunate
than you.

Remember that
though receiving gifts
is a lot of fun,
It is not the most
important part.

Because the spirit of Christmas

is mostly about

Having a kind and generous heart.